AF138899

...to Ruby

Naked
in the
Coffee House

Selected Poems

Robert Grant

Bibliographische Information der Deutschen Nationalbibliothek: Die Deutsche Nationalbibliothek verzeichnet diese Publikation in der Deutschen Nationalbibliographie; detaillierte bibliographische Daten sind im Internet über www.dnb.de abrufbar.

Herstellung und Verlag:

BoD – Books on Demand, Norderstedt

ISBN   978-3-7392-0190-0

Contents

**Facebook Status Update,
June 27th 2015, 4.12 am**

*I run my hands through what brain I
have left and thankfully still come up
with something more interesting than
weather reports. Drunk in my favorite
Berlin bar, writing nonsense to no one.*

Ellipses

There's a guy sat in front of me
watching porn on his laptop,
in a coffee shop
whilst eating a breakfast muffin.

Everyone around him is ignoring
the fact that it's just so obvious.
About as obvious as the fact
that I'm sat behind him, writing about it.

Just as I'm watching
the exhausted mother
staring into the space
where her imagination used to be.

The older couple
still so into each other

laughing loudly, as no work tomorrow
just drinking today.

A confused tourist
servicing rendered opinions,
guided by failed novelists
and bartenders alike.

The expressive talker
gesturing wildly,
no doubt making some fatuous point
that even she doesn't fully understand.

The middle aged middle manager
power suit, lime green tie. Numb look
slapped across his face, head against the
window dreaming about painting
or some interesting alternative.

As

More people enter
through the amazingly small door,
which hits the fake leather seat back
annoying Mr. businessman's coffee
all over his tie.

By

The spunky hipsters,
striding with thick black rimmed glasses
confident, beautiful,
yet ignorant to their acoustic level.

This is a place where reality
is found
coffee served, break ups announced,
dreams crushed.

Missing only, an arrogant poet,
slumped in the corner

watching another man'*s* porn

writing ellipses,

with an erection.

Temporal tin pot

...and so it begins again.

Thoughts corroding reasons,

reasons sculptured into distortions

Rorschach impressions of life.

The past has been drawn to this point

now consuming the present

with future possibilities

fragmenting any want to continue

in any form of now.

For what is, Now?

Is now the experience you are having in

this present tense?

But by thinking about it in this way

are we not changing the present

making a new construction of now.

So is it true to say that I am temporal?
Temporally controlled
by knowledge of my past.
Therefore, time is moving
in both directions and is no more
than a conduit of experience.

If I choose to get run over by a car,
drink a beer, smoke a cigarette.

The past effects the present
in the same way as the present
effects the future,
for time is merely an illusion,
existence is all there ever has or ever
will be, striding toward a memory
of even writing this.

Do I stop here?

                    ...or here?

Or continue writing until the ink runs
clear
              paper becomes extinct.

Do I stop mid-sentence...
                    ...to simply confuse.

If time be truly temporal and there is
<u>only</u> this moment existing purely
in the mind.

Then maybe this poem
should go on forever
and we should all fuck,
extremely slowly.

Naked

What will this world have me do,
when it's ripped off my skin
left me standing naked in the night,
watching monochrome moments
in free fall,
as I spin towards infinity
rejecting the man
I see on reflection.

When all I have to show
for a life spent dreaming are;
liver spot on back of hand
black spots rampantly surfacing
when conflicted thoughts
come to running once more,
a motley parade of mimicry
behind blanket walls of tear.

When we've locked all hopes of solution
in that black plasma box
adorning my bed room,
adorning my heart,
swallowing down the key
whilst most bent in knee
as they take away my vanity
pumping hard from behind.

When all it really comes down to
are cheapened version of sanity,
credit card solutions
for greeting card holidays,
nothing more or less than
a 21st century one world state
punching feed bars for pellets
in suburban shopping malls.

When sometimes I think
they've got it right,

those terrorists freedom birds
standing to put up a fight,
giving us back the same hardship
we gave them first,
screaming
'GOD WILL SAVE US ALL'
as we burst forth
our superior fighting force
and blow the skins of children
playing football in the park.

When opinion is no longer counted,
no one stands up,
no one starts shouting
we all just sit silent,
gag mouthed in solitude
because we don't want to rock the boat
shake the tree,
say anything to allude
to our true feelings.

When all I can do is write a few words
down, for preacher corner audiences
on a Monday
just before noon,
when all the people that really should
be listening, are locked in cattle cars
whoring out their lives
so fat men may grows fatter.

When every day is a question of
motivation, of relevant ambition,
so closed to where
we really should be
we walk, face to the floor,
listening intently to successes
rehashing other peoples fantastic
experiences.

When the alternative generation
hides in bog standard impressions,

those individual expressions
coming from H&M with a receipt
a name on my feet,
brand stamped across my heart.

When all I can hope
is that a word or two seep in,
a rhyme hits land on a shore,
so far from where we really should be
that the concept of normality is lost.

What will this world have me do,

but stand, naked in this night,

raped of imagination,

with energy only

to ask why.

Naturally manmade

...then it fell quiet.
Pond skaters
only dancing
when he looks their way.

Humming cars,
silenced by a thought
bumbling in his belly, as
cigarettes wrestle his gag reflex
due to this forced,
man-made serenity.

Birds make no sound,
but for that of mating rituals
played through a broken phonograph
in a distance, constructed purely of song.

Whistled from
small child's swallows,
then thrown back up
in disgust of the noise,
those noises more
affirmation than ritualistic.

Fish flip their tails,
absolving themselves
from petty arguments
put forth by a large seagull
turned instantly to dragonfly,
purely for acoustic effect.

For this is a quiet place,
a man made serenity
too constructed to be natural,
too symmetrical to be accidental,
a twenty-first century version
of how calm really should seam.

The illusion dispelled,

the lie protruding,

he sits and vomits reaction

breaking forced silence,

if silence was ever there

to be broken at all.

Baby Love

Oh, wasted youth.

Spoilt, but for the love of a child.

First find your own voice,

before teaching others to speak

In time to drink

I'm destroying myself.
Becoming a parody of everything I think
I should be.
Sinking any real reason to consider
myself anything than what I have
become. That being,
a drunk!

Now it has to stop.
For words will not fall onto the page
by themselves.
Poems won't be written by
he who thinks that by simply saying,
makes it so. For,
I'm a drunk.

Tell yourself in the morning

that today I will write.
For when the urge comes again
and it will, put down the bottle and
find my rare, dare to be great moment
of clarification, not
coffee shop pantomime.

This tide of wallow
now resides in hollow sentiment,
these thoughts of preconceived greatness
now rest in twitching arms,
as days turn to weeks
and yet more great poems
reside firmly in my bowls.

Honesty lives in the true parts of this lie.
In small moments of lucidity,
when you know you are doing
something you should not. That
spilt second at the end of the night,

when you realize
you've had too much.

As you tumble through the same streets,
confessing sins in monologue,
tripping on the pavement, ending up
face down in a pool of freshest Berlin
dog piss. Standing to confess
change ideas, find a sink and kick
the next dog I see firmly in the balls!

Take away these foolish whims to live in
the eyes of poets past. Move forward to
glance upon the world with honest eyes,
with reasons to do, rather than say have
done. Hold tight, never to let go of a
mind, so nearly confined to history
by a bottle of whisky and past success.

I'm undone.

Still unmade.

Yet my mind would have me think

otherwise,

my liver the same,

as I tap out these few words

in time to drink.

The difference between musicians and poets

I once gave my book and pen
to a well known musician friend
after a show.
Asked him to write down a thought,
expecting something profound.

He drew a picture of a penis
ejaculating over a woman's back.

I sat, pondered,
then realised,
that in one insignificant scribble, he had
expressed the emotion he was feeling
at that very moment.

It really was the only thing on his mind
at that moment in time.

He then took one of his fans and
did exactly what he drew.
Thus proving,
life to be really that simple to extract
for some people.

A day later he confirmed to me that she
had called asking for more of the same.

As I now sit, watching birds skim
catching flies in a blooming spring park,
finding words with which to tell this
interlude, relationship benevolence
can be my only conclusion.

For I must at least understand a woman,
before I blow my load over her back.

Black Cat

One meter

from

the coffee house door,

lays a dead

black cat.

But that's

a lie.

For he lives loudly,

in my

dead head.

Basketball

They stretch their backs.

Clamped hands behind their head,

for the twist.

A basketball is picked and passed,

back n forth.

Bravado smoked then expelled

with the alpha arch.

Legs becoming contorted into strange

positions, which really can't be

that healthy.

Pounded chests glowing red,

as the street girl circulate aroma.

Piss kissing circles in the air towards

their men so beautiful in the sun.

Corrupting one to break from the herd.

Becoming encircled by the attention

rivals, so soft, so delicate.

His mammals pull him back in,

with a manly mating cry's of

"John…what the fuck? Let's play ball"

He proudly rejoins, shoulders back,

stiff with machismo.

The ball is thrown his way

and all is forgotten.

The games is on.

First shot sails high and wide,

as does second and third.

Then, posturing, running,

a two handed bounce pass

and two more failed shots.

The females grow weary,

not seeing their men here present.

Only seeing fools

who can't play basket ball,

shrouded in mistrust

of affirmed intentions.

This dance culminated

in the silver back,

with the newest backwards cap.

Stretching the 'Wilson' back calling

"Watch this one girls!"

His testicles released high into the air,

so cocky, so sure.

It sails high and clear

through a beautiful sky,

arching as if thrown by Hades himself.

His feet touch ground

yet continue to dance.

Hand flopped, on locked elbow.

Slowing slightly to see the ball...

...totally miss the back board, ending up
about five feet behind in a gaunt bush.

His face imploded, his bounce, halted.
He opens his mouth just one more time,
reaffirming status
with five iconic words.

"Fuck this...let's play baseball"

The inevitable coffee

He sits, like most mornings,

alone but for a pen

and a clean white page.

Thinking why and how,

even sometimes when.

Of what happens, now all has happened.

Next; a baby cries

coffee cups are dropped

and bedlam ensues

on the opposite side

of a coffee house

at the corner Hufeland and Esmarch Str.

An engaging look comes his way,

a wink, whisper.

Enter dog,

enter second time mother,

enter expressions of frustration,

on face of grizzled child.

An enticing leg cross,

follow glance,

enter past chapter

he thinks and smokes,

for that avenue is happily closed.

Turn away, look away, sips to smirk.

A head turn and cough follow.

Seeing a mirror outside, showing a man

with a guitar, note book in hand.

Frustrating the air, for words just won't

come, pouting incessantly

in the mid morning sun.

He soon realises;

that time will always move on,

people will always grow slightly older,
coffee cups
will always be dropped,
arguments always ensue.

He finally sees, in the cacophony,
that life is no more
than a procession forward, toward
the inevitability of questions,
to the end of coffee mornings,
the outing of religious lies.

He finally sees the world
through every persons eyes.
Then sits thinking,
returning to his original thought.
Enlightened by symmetry
and cheeky female retort.

Harmison

"The crazy days
are over now,
Harmison

It's time
to grow up.

The fucking
has stopped,

the drinking
has stopped,

the passion
has stopped,

Harmison,
this makes
no sense.

For Harmison
is dead"

How to:
Chat up a writer

"Want to get a drink?" She,
the pop eyed blonde said to me,
as I sit, one eyeing the bar in stagger.

"I am a dirty cynical bastard" I
reply, with a half smile of half teeth."I'm
looking for something more than a sound
bite, dot com existence" I continue.
"Want, just once, to feel something that
hasn't been said or done before"

"So, you're a writer?" question
comes, her glinted twinkle fading.

"I started writing poetry many
years ago now" I state "Under the
illusion that it would get the emotions
out of my head. Locked onto a page
forever in time and fate, so some bendy

teenagers can look at it, after I'm gone.
And understand that I was just like them,
at one point. The world in which I live
has been used up, already spat out by
me, poetry slammers and greeting cards.
The people I meet, in this pained
existence, swim past, never quite
touching land, so wrapped in a black
blanket, that they feel warm enough to
smile from time to time. I only smile
when I'm drunk or writing. Both
commodities, always under or over used.
I can't see which anymore. Can't see the
grey between black and black, feel the
reason between wrong and wrong.
People often ask me what it's like to be a
writer, as if it's some choice that I've
made, as if it's some rational decision
based on economic fact. When all it
really is, is a life filled with bad choices

and unfaithfulness. It's just great! I always say, freedom of speech, the right to say what I think. Self absorbed arsehole, slumped on a dirty bar, looking for another drink, but it's funny how often those things, go hand in hand" I add with a wink. "So smile at me and buy me just one more round, I'll tell you story of love and times in my past when the city made sense, back when everything was sound. A great man, far greater than me, simply said 'Born into this' I can only agree, then try to do something original! So to the end of my sad little tale and back to the original question. Do you want to fuck me or slap me, as I don't kiss ass or talk small."

She was deeply unimpressed.

Twitchy

A twitchy morning,

don't believe myself today

need to clear the chamber, break the egg

disturb some coffee, twitch a little

sit in the streets of Berlin, dressed,

figure some things through,

eat bread, brush my hair n teeth,

sit up straight, remember to slouch

wrestle with ideas and voices, wonder

why and how I've come to be

sitting here…twitching

pondering on the rest of the day

as that pain snaps through my arm

and I'm left helpless at a keyboard

wishing my typing skills were better,

smile at the beggar man

drink with simpletons

reduce myself to their level,

sit haggard and hungry

let out into evening by the

calls of the perverted

the kind who fuck in nightclub stalls

only asking questions

whilst putting their pants back on,

exude flamboyance

don't settle the bar tab

or explain the reasoning

behind drunken statements,

for that is what you're getting

by being close to me

the twitchy one,

with blood shot eyes and loud coughs

the vagrant one,

who shouts for attention from any

woman, for

he doesn't think he's fucked enough yet

if that's what you want?

the twitchy one,

a distraction

an unwanted flyer for 50% off pizza

shoved into your mouth,

then left to fester

becoming sodden

by sputum and

other ejaculates,

If you want,

       him

          me

            us

              the twitchy one

then I'm right here baby.

Danielle

Accused with no return to sanity.

Never knowing why,

nor the need to be known.

You ask the questions,

I smile innocently

heartbroken, misunderstood emotions.

Leaving a taste,

not known before this day,

why is all the want, to

think of me in this way.

Tarnished by your misconception

bruising with hurt,

ripening from deepest pain.

Projected emptiness,

sending my soul spinning

questioning self, like never before.

Innocence, replacing confidence,
as I reason with my mind.
For you don't know me, you never will,
to even think I could be so ill.

Once thought feelings of love
now changed to misconstrued
emotional hatred.
For you have damaged me more
than I ever thought to do to you.
This now ending friendship
controlled by your betrayal
of one like me.

You'll never feel my warmth,
never feel my sex
never see my eyes on a flower morning.
For now has gone,
never to return.
Another will feel my hug,

feel my eyes wrapping the pain
of this spinning orb.
Humanity confused by television,
you...by me?

So why did this have to happen?
After all the drinking,
laughing sunny days.
If this is what you needed to get by,
well at least I've been able to do
something wondrous.
My needful arms,
now wrapped around another,
the past smiling secretive smiles.

Future opening forward,
days switch to nights
sparkling tears to my ambition,
leaving, the dust on you,
blowing up the future of me.

You now stand behind my eyes forever,

to look upon this world and say,

we were so close, once.

Caffeine dreams

Pushed down
in the corner of the store,
you sit jealously
drawing the others out.

Chromed hood
hiding dependence,
in steamed haze
and fashionable chatter.

They sit around you,
as you file their caffeine needs
with biscotti
and pop news.

They, attempting to be interesting
Sit devouring

a plethora of nonsense
processed food.

Not seeing that
their original way
Is no more individual
than eating at McDonalds.

Open Mic

I arrive early.

Just me and

the bartender

chatting

about

Jazz,

as he

pours me

a large,

beer.

Then,

in walks

the owner.

Ignores me

at first,

whilst gauging

my mood and if
he will have to
throw me out
later.

Soon, the bar swells.
Swaying under
the weight of
five bad guitarist,
two lounge singers,
a transgender cabaret dancer
and the
obligatory
nervous
comedians.

The host
arrives
taking names,
as I

consider

my surroundings,

take another

beer

and begin

deflecting small talk .

Show starts

with a

large Scandinavian

singer-songwriter

who

can do neither

thing, follow

comedian,

follow

clown.

Then a break.

Stereo pumped,

nodding heads

chatter

to old

Pearl Jam

songs

as drinks

flow

hot 'n' hard.

Break done.

The next comedian

shoots himself

in the head.

Rape joke, not

sitting well

with anyone.

Receiving jibes and whispers

from the women

at the front.

He leaves the stage

to no applause,

through a

room of

misconception.

Fingering the air

for his

'performers'

free

beer.

Takes a seat.

Looks at me.

"Tough crowd"

he says,

ego smashed.

I nod, he sinks

and sips,

the next

will be up soon,

he hopes.

A flat-chested,

heavily tattooed

guitarist,

starts passing off

obscure

cover versions

as her own.

I'm left

quietly

inebriated.

Surrounded by

hobbyist

the hopeful,

embittered

bar staff

and the misguided.

Left wondering

which

category

I fall in to.

This horror closes

on the host,

rapping

rhyming slogans

of next weeks

show.

I just gather

my cigarettes

and slip quietly

into the night.

Girl

One night after a show,
a girl approached.
Manuscript in hand
pensive gaze, fixed.

"Can you read this? Let me know
what you think" she asked and ran. © &
email as header of each crumpled page.

Over morning coffee, in
my favourite dispensary.
I read on,
expected naivety.

'Fate is a roundabout with only one exit'
Her opener.

Followed by;

'Loneliness is a balaclava with no eye holes'

        Then;

'Sex is an exercise. Making love is a confirmation of intention'

All under the banner 'Haikus'

I sent a pleasant email
that very morning.
Explaining her
simple mistake.

She replied
with the title line
'Misogynistic Prick'
and photo of her middle finger.

I'm pleased I never saw her again.

Famously

Fame is a flatulent hemorrhoid
on the arse of humanity.

Worn flamboyantly red
by years of supposed
glamour and razzmatazz.

Gone are our romantic hero's,
replaced with financial chintz
and medically altered beauties.

We watch on with internet eyes,
seeing the truly talent less
become interesting.

The irrational become financial.
Reality television becoming

so much more than oxymoron.

We consume our need to be thin
and beautiful, because we're neither
or they will have us believe.

Not heroes, so they can sell
us theirs, not remarkable,
but they have the cure.

These piranhas,
sit, waiting for pockets to be striped.
Boned of stiff spine and imagination.

But, we have put them there,
pedestaled and radiant,
because we thought we needed them,
thought we had to in order to survive.

Therefore, only we can tear them down,

only we can replace

these giant golden pigs,

these kings of profiteering

with the real masters

of our present universe.

So let's make THIS generation

BEAT in our heart.

Not downloaded but experienced

THIS eras talent,

paraded on our shoulders,

for all to relish.

Live true

and never trust anyone,

who acts like they're famous.

On a train

Small reminders of where I'm from,
the train rattles my brain into action.
These boys made men by experience
before me
stand, to let plugged women rest.

I sit badger winged,
sabre sheathed by my side pain,
vibrated awake
by uneven track shoes.
As we wobble down
the rails of aging.

So jazzed to be here,
yet still ensure how, in the blink
of one pink eye
we have turned to the aged.

Protruding from youth
as if made as accompaniment
to ice cream.

Our memories alluding us,
resting head on shoulder
when hipsters expel energy.
Hoping to catch a remnant
in panting mouth,
this dog breathed commander waits.

To see if this girl has fantasies
or if that guy will ever smile.
Observe, that she wants him hard.
I think he's gay, but appreciates
the compliment.

The punk and priest
sharing a bench seat
reading over each other shoulders

of religion and speed rock,

after hard days at the office,

glad to be on their way home.

All these distractions

compressed into one drop of sweat

now beading down my forehead.

Leaving me nauseous from the effort

of writing on a train.

Joshua 153

I must

break

away

from this

Youtube

existence,

this

multimedia

strife.

Before life

begins flashing,

like so many

doctored clips

on my

very own

pointless

reality

television

show.

Sitting for hours

thinking

it's ok,

because I'm watching

documentaries

or sport replays.

Ending my day

in a half blind

blur, trying

hard to remember

what I've done.

I sit unwashed,

this, Berlin

immigrant bum,

pumping clip after clip

of the same

pedaled tedium.

Hour upon hour

of stationary advance,

towards an

immunized state

deep down south in

procrastination country.

I must summit to

submission guidelines.

Talk to strangers about nothing.

Hold friends closer, expel the chaff

like a used fag butt.

But wait now, distracted,

pop up post of some tired lady

attempting to jump off

the old Brooklyn bridge.

Mind arrested, curiosity suggested,

but I wonder what else

is on the channel

of Joshua 153.

The Poets

I sit in a room of poets,

talking about literature.

When it suddenly (Although not

suddenly at all) occurs to me

that I am surrounded

by the problem with modern literature.

They all hate me,

as I won't play their game

won't engage in their frivolity.

That peacocking display

that always happens

at events like these.

They talk and talk,

I simply sit and listen

nodding my head from time to time

to show I'm still engaged,

whilst festering in the need

to show their horrifying similarities.

Show them that the women

sat to the left of me

just said exactly the same (I learnt this

construction in university)

as the guy sat to the right of me.

They flex literary shoulders

in order to impress the people

who've flocked,

the problem being

that as long as these farcical similarities

sit flexing their shoulders

in order to swoon,

nothing new will be discovered.

Poetic notions have infested

my drinking space.

I am becoming drowsy,

even angry.

As these hallow attempts sit

making interesting conversation points,

with no more order

than to shake literary tail feathers.

Those feathers should be plucked,

one by one from their unoriginal asses

and made into a brightly colored

head dress.

So that everyone, for miles around,

can see that the poets are in town

then return home to wash face and hands

of that same stayed, pedaled bullshit.

I sit quietly, drinking,

watching those feathers

fluttering in a slight westerly breeze

from the open dark wood door,

realizing fully that these opinions

are only mine

and at truly the best of times

opinionated.

Quickly replacing my beer glass

on the table.

Then picking up my coat,

to leave.

Well walked...

...into many coffee shops

on many street corners,

so many times

that I've now forgotten.

Feeling those eyes upon me

somehow trouser-less, spanked.

Ostentatious nights,

tinder box promises,

disgracefully opulent morning strolls

through the expensive quarter.

Under watered

'n' miles away from

any form of struggle.

One minute meltdown

Somewhere in my head
I feel comfortable
with what I'm doing.
Find validation
in the words I write.

This dirty moneyless crime
I'm committing.
Facet of guarded truth,
loosened belt buckle
compulsion.

Returning with neat re-invention
comprehending only faked
conclusions are untrue.
Looking down to see,
exactly what you expect, is a blessing.

Many confuse this with
a pariahs wish to be popular.
An unnecessary reaction
to an unmasked assumption,
reverberating conclusions with haste.

For they see a mad women,
buck toothed and hideous.
Head, hid in a corner, told to by teacher.
Sneering tasteless reactions like an
impatient damp dog, waiting
for its ball to be thrown.

From that point on, becoming
absorbed by the power pursuit.
Sharply realising one morning
with a twitch and a stroke
that, that wasted life they held so dearly,
has ended in the most blasé way.

That's all she sang or thought she sang
or wrote or whistled through the lips of a
Mexican stag bull,
that time that never
really happened, but it did,
never did!

Distracted by passing shapes
or contact killers
sent in just to rumble the fantasy,
so erroneous,
it now sits in your haggard memory
twitching it's foreskin
with a cocaine soiled credit card.

Chilli

I just scratched my nose
after cutting chillies. Then,
from the stupidity of it,
rubbed my eyes in horror.

Beginning to enjoy the pain
a little too much
I thought about
masturbating.

Twenty minutes after
and for the rest of the day
I sat in a plastic bowl filled with yogurt,
which was fun too.

Heater

We're trapped into a form of life
that cannot be taught,
can't be learnt,
stretched or moulded into
something it's not.
At the base of thought
with purest form,
it's perfect.

When executed,
its style is unbounded
by questions and reasons,
putting forth explanations
to roads less travelled
or a crazy night,
confined after to a bed
with a cold.

Tissues cascading

over the floor,

slotted together,

bringing corrosive arrangements

to dance, in ore of

an incestuous need to

create oneself over

in word.

Ejaculating the first misfire of

mindless retort,

posed by a fool.

Left festering awake,

as you beat him over the head

with drab memories

of that time once

when you should have done it.

Standing in an ankle deep bathtub

holding a four bar heater,

hoping someone can stop

the monologue.

Pen hitting page,

expelling truth

with flow,

untold and unmentioned.

Quiet moments

of contemplative sanity

lost, tossed through

madness mistakes

and missteps,

by a hand

that knows no salvation

from imagination.

Muddied waters

break on this shore,

lapping over crippled feet,

I stand eroded.

Barricading my soft spot

with a handmade

façade of tranquillity.

For this is now my madness,

my untaught curse.

Urging my finger to relax their grasp,

so I may see oblivion

with enough juice,

to fire up Wisconsin.

Porn star?

I have all the outward appearances

of being a normal functioning

member of society.

All the attributes of a successful life.

Nice flat,

new clothes,

money in my pocket.

I fear I would be judged differently

if observed a little more closely.

For you would see

the abused boy I once was.

The, now tired, house broken

father I have become.

As rushed as

my dumpling faced cherub,

to grow up.

As loud minded

as my expensive cars exhaust,

falsely flamboyant

as that new babies clothes.

When you look closely enough

at anyone or anything,

you can clearly see the cracks.

See the mistakes

woven into the sidewalk.

Left as exposed as

a porn stars asshole

in a double penetration scene.

Exhausted after,

with a pocket full of money

and cum on my shoes.

If you look closely enough at me.

Down, to the Monday morning questions

after Saturday night expressions.

If you could see that man, that bum,

the mime would slip and a

far more normal human would stand.

Only to tip his hat,

quickly fading away,

leaving a flaming

thought at your feet

for stamping.

A little
piece of nonsense

There are a thousand things
I could be doing right now,
most of them not involving
sitting in my coffee shop
drinking coffee.

More to do with me writing something,
but then, isn't that exactly
what I'm doing?

So I'm complaining about doing
exactly what, I am (in fact) doing.
Sitting, thinking about having
a cigarette, maybe
walking around a little,
stopping somewhere else

in order to drink more coffee and smoke.

Thus, actually achieving
what I set out on the path
in the first place.

So maybe there is some point
to me sitting in a posh coffee house,
drinking sour lattes
surrounded by arsehole.
Blending in perfectly
as I'm one of them.

The so nearly man

The so nearly man sits in
a dank, single room
attempting to write himself interesting.
Attempting to write away
from the choices he has made.
His novel, "Much more" was
so nearly published.

The phone rings, it's Carol, his ex,
telling him how her father just died
and the pain is building.
He commiserates,
replacing the receiver to
cry for exactly two minutes, they
so nearly made it.

He imagines across the roof tops

of Spanish villages in sunlight

as the strip bar neon's flutter,

whores argue,

smells from the fry shop permeate the air

and a beer is located,

cracked then drank from

a half crumpled can, he

so nearly could afford Gin.

Belly hanging over belt,

folding patterns into

his ever greying flesh.

Feet sit crippled in

sweating plastic shoes

framed by polyester socks

purchased from

a supermarket checkout line. He

so nearly had leather loafers.

He stands to wander

around a hellish reality,

talking briskly to no friends

about the estranged life

he seems to have created.

Hands conducting the air

to a crescendo of silence, as

once more, his charisma

tells him to be still. He

so nearly had vigour and might.

The so nearly man

returns to drinking,

aware of his genius,

his foibles and folly,

knowing full that he

so nearly lived his life.

The Monday
after Sunday night

I walk in circles.
Wishing myself
more beautiful.

Wishing myself
away from the rules,
so imprinted.

Visions return
from
vacant shop windows.

Conducting
cold air to oust,
this vapid id.

This,

dreamscape psychology

so pumped, postured.

Punching self

with drunken arms,

amid shrunken head.

More personalities

present

than needed.

Circles to spinning,

masquerading the majestic.

for the radiant bum has returned.

Spinning becomes saying,

a thousand words a minute,

speed chatting scenarios of care.

Morning coffee commuters,
conversing in sign language.
Sit gesturing their indifference.

Spinning completed,
come wink, come wit,
as I continue about my day.

Leaving sour tastes
on the lips of the hunted,
inside their herded parade.

The art
of being homeless

Why do artists

of any description, feel the need

to abuse themselves so much.

Whether it be with booze or weed

or both, whether it gets stronger than

that, why?

You see artists are like the homeless

there's always something else on their

mind. Traipsing through a rainy day

with memories trapped in plastic bags

by their sides,

their only relevant ambition being

to find somewhere called home.

Both finding crowds confining,

better off alone.

For when by themselves

both segments the same

no party to crash, nobody to blame,

this is when they feel most comfortable.

There's a homeless guy

lives in a doorway down my street.

Always same tired expression

same constant frown,

no sentence to say

just sparse random sound

of a life spent dreaming.

I would take pity

throw down a coin

for coffee or beer, if

I wasn't so fucking scared that

I'll be down there

this time, next year.

Stones from a balcony

He's the man that stands before you
and the man that's already left.
He knows what you're thinking
and why you're thinking that way.

For he is the child throwing stones from
a balcony, a baby crying in the coffee
shop. An attracter of unwanted attention
whilst working through emotional
content.

Split into fractions, awaiting
reunification, for without conflict he is
nothing more than simple train wreck.
A couplet reaction to an unanswered
question, simulating tension with ease.

This is how he can be in two places at
once. His reputation precedes him,
lingering long after he's left, confirming
the fact that maybe, too many people
have been let in too far or so they think.

People have always come and gone
through his life. Laughing loudly and
drinking by his side. Then when out
shouted becoming scared to continue
and running.

Which of his faces you are drinking with
is all dependent on which of his faces
you know to be his,
and in which company
you've been kept.

You don't know the man that stands
before you, or the man that has already

left. But he knows what he's thinking and why he's thinking that way.